Enfolded in God's Arms

Also by Lisa Aré Wulf

Reaching for God's Hand
40 Reflections to Deepen Your Faith Journey

On a Quest for Christ
Tracing the Footsteps of Your Spiritual Journey

Silent Moments with God Series

Enfolded in God's Arms

40 Reflections to
Embrace Your Inner Healing

Lisa Aré Wulf

Spiritual Formation House™
Colorado Springs, Colorado
www.spiritualformationhouse.com

Scripture quotations marked (NIV) are taken from THE HOLY BIBLE, NEW INTERNATIONAL VERSION®, NIV® Copyright © 1973, 1978, 1984, 2011 by Biblica, Inc.® Used by permission. All rights reserved worldwide.

Scripture quotations marked (NLT) are taken from the Holy Bible, New Living Translation, copyright © 1996, 2004, 2007 by Tyndale House Foundation. Used by permission of Tyndale House Publishers, Inc., Carol Stream, Illinois 60188. All rights reserved.

Two sermon illustrations used by permission of the Rev. Denson F. Freeman Jr.

Cover Design by Jennifer Burrell - Fresh Vision Design
Interior Design by Wood Nymph Creations
Cover Photograph by Kim (Fotolia)
Personal Photograph by Katie Corinne Photography

Publisher's Cataloging-in-Publication data

Names: Wulf, Lisa Aré, author.
Title: Enfolded in God's arms : 40 reflections to embrace your inner healing / Lisa Aré Wulf.
Series: Silent Moments with God Series.
Description: Colorado Springs, CO: Spiritual Formation House, 2016.
Identifiers: ISBN 978-1-938042-07-2 (Hardcover) | 978-1-938042-02-7 (Pbk.) | 978-1-938042-03-4 (Kindle) | 978-1-938042-09-6 (eBook) | 978-1-938042-10-2 (Audio) | LCCN 2016907065
Subjects: LCSH Christian life--Devotional literature. | Bible--Meditations. | Christian life--Meditations. | Devotional exercises. | BISAC Religion / Christian Life / Devotional
Classification: LCC BV4832.2 W84 2016 | DDC 242.2--dc23

Published by Spiritual Formation House™
3154 Vickers Dr.
Colorado Springs, CO 80918
www.spiritualformationhouse.com

Printed in the United States of America

To all who seek healing

Contents

A Time to Grow

Acknowledgements

I am delighted to thank these very special friends whose contributions and support for this book have been invaluable:

My fabulous editor, Kim McCauley, whose expertise, patience, and friendship were indispensable to this effort.

My two great test readers, Jan Malvern and Jerusha Goebel, whose insights and encouragement refined and shaped this offering.

My excellent proofreader, Susan Defosset, whose eagle eye carefully combed through every inch of the manuscript.

My wonderful husband, Calvin, for his sage advice, encouragement, and patience through endless readings and conversation.

Thanks to each one. This book has become a reality because of you!

The Journey Begins

There is a time for everything,
and a season for every activity under the heavens.
Ecclesiastes 3:1 (NIV)

The rhythm of creation flows through seasons. We know them well—spring, summer, fall, and winter. They revisit us year after year. Many of us have our favorites and also those we don't particularly like.

We find the rhythm of seasons in our own lives too. Various seasons repeat. Some intensely happy or difficult seasons appear only once. Today, we may walk in a period of deep satisfaction and joy. Later, our days may be filled with struggle and sorrow. There is a season for every activity under heaven.

The season of healing is especially tender. It is a time of flux and searching, pain and growth. It may feel as if we are making progress, only to find ourselves stepping back into a prior struggle. But we're not floundering. Rather, this may be how God chooses to work in our lives during this season.

Enfolded in God's Arms: 40 Reflections to Embrace Your Inner Healing is part of the Silent Moments with God series addressing key areas in the lives of those seeking God. This book contains forty devotionals, gathered into four sections:

A Time to Heal
A Time to Change
A Time with Jesus
A Time to Grow

Each reflection begins with a scripture verse, followed by a short devotional and a few questions to ponder. An excerpt from a Psalm and a brief prayer are also included. As the reflection ends, take a moment to journal the truth of your own life experience.

Don't miss the special section in every chapter called, "Be Still for a Silent Moment with God." It's important to pause during each reflection and sit quietly. Open your mind to hear what God may say to you.

Embarking on a healing journey may take courage—lots of courage. But where will it come from? Can you summon it up from the depths of your being? You may find this type of courage simply arises from holding tightly to God's hand. As each of us travels our sometimes smooth and sometimes rocky path, Jesus is our constant companion—a friend who never wavers, who always guides and encourages us.

As you begin your journey, hold these words of Scripture in your heart:

"Do not fear, for I have redeemed you;
I have summoned you by name; you are mine.
When you pass through the waters,
I will be with you;
and when you pass through the rivers,
they will not sweep over you.
When you walk through the fire,
you will not be burned;
the flames will not set you ablaze.
For I am the LORD, your God,
the Holy One of Israel, your Savior…"
Isaiah 43:1b–3a (NIV)

I wish you a journey filled with healing, hope, and happiness.

A Time to Heal

૭

Is it time to change and
stop trying to measure up?

The Phone Call

All that the Father gives me will come to me,
and whoever comes to me I will never drive away.
John 6:37 (NIV)

I'm still waiting. Why doesn't the phone ring? I keep it by my side and continually check my messages. Will the call ever come?

As far back as I can remember, I knew I wasn't good enough. My life was spent trying to jump over a bar that seemed to be set ever higher. All I wanted was to make the grade and be acceptable. But somehow that never happened.

Perhaps you struggle like this too. Are you waiting for a phone call from someone close to you, hoping they will say you measure up now, that you can stop trying so hard? Unfortunately, a reality check says that's probably not going to happen.

Actually, it shouldn't happen. Trying to be good enough is a symptom of flawed theology. If our goal is to live by faith, then wanting to be "good enough" doesn't really fit. It implies that God's love for us is conditional, and we must constantly pass a test in order to be acceptable.

There's another issue too. When we put so much emphasis on being okay, then everything is about us instead of God. When we focus on ourselves, God is consigned to a small, dusty corner of our lives, a demotion he's probably not too pleased about!

Perhaps you and I have been waiting for the wrong phone call. The real call—the only call—was made centuries ago. The message from Jesus said, "I have redeemed you; you are mine."

Hear my prayer, LORD;
listen to my cry for mercy.
When I am in distress, I call to you,
because you answer me.
Psalm 86:6–7 (NIV)

Be Still
for a
Silent Moment with God

Digging Deeper

What phone call are you waiting for?

Why is this call important to you?

How could you switch the connection to God's phone?

Prayer for Today

I've spent too many years tied to my phone, hoping to hear that I've made the grade. I didn't believe I was okay in your eyes either, God. Help me see how wrong I've been. It's time to change and stop trying to measure up. Be with me as I finally accept your love. Amen.

Your Thoughts

❧

Could there be a different perspective
on our circumstances?

Dismount

*For I am the LORD your God
who takes hold of your right hand and says to you,
Do not fear; I will help you.
Isaiah 41:13 (NIV)*

"When you discover you're riding a dead horse, the best strategy is to dismount." This statement, attributed to ancient Dakota Indian lore, holds much wisdom for those who feel stuck in life.

Why is it so hard for us to dismount when areas of our lives clearly aren't working? Do we not see what's happening? Are we afraid to make a change? Do we insist that this time it will work out? Perhaps all of the above!

When we find ourselves in such a situation, the first step is to pull up the reins, stop, and observe what's going on.

Why do we react the way we do? Could there be a different perspective on our circumstances?

As you begin to quiet your fears, bravely gaze deep inside your soul. There you can discover clues to your quandary and how to move forward. But you need a hand to hold, a gentle guide for your steps. Perhaps that hand belongs to Jesus.

Where is he? He may speak through a friend who quietly listens and helps. Or he himself may whisper in your ear as he holds you close, "It's time to dismount."

Are you ready to get off the horse? Here's all you need to do. Mentally swing one leg behind you to the ground. Then release your other foot from the stirrup. You'll find yourself on firm terrain with a fresh perspective, ready to walk with Jesus in an exciting new direction.

Lead me by your truth and teach me,
for you are the God who saves me.
All day long I put my hope in you.
Psalm 25:5 (NLT)

Be Still
for a
Silent Moment with God

Digging Deeper

Is there something you should stop doing but you don't think you can? What is it?

How could you begin to look at your situation from a new angle?

In what ways could God give you the strength to make changes?

Prayer for Today

Sometimes I feel like I'm moving fast yet going nowhere. But I can't seem to stop. I need your guidance and protection, God. Give me the strength to stop what I'm doing, turn around, and follow your lead. More than anything, I want to walk with you today, tomorrow, and forever. Amen.

Your Thoughts

⚮

We want others to think we're doing great
and have all the answers to life.

REFLECTION 3

Reality Shows

The LORD doesn't see things the way you see them.
People judge by outward appearance,
but the LORD looks at the heart.
1 Samuel 16:7b (NLT)

I once read an article about whether reality shows on television are actually real. Not surprisingly, the answer was no! Apparently, most reality shows are staged and even recorded several times. So, what is being portrayed as reality…isn't!

Being rather trusting and naïve, I tend to believe the image someone portrays is genuine. Then I begin to wonder why that person appears to be so much more "together" than me. But are others really more organized, more confident, more spiritually mature? Or could they be just as uncertain and unsure as I am?

Of course, there's another side to this story. Many of us are experts at putting on a good face. We want people to think we're doing great and have all the answers to life—or at least most of the important ones. But perhaps we're merely playing the same game on each other.

Where is God in all this? Does he care how our "reality shows" look to others? Probably not. Even though he knows the real truth about us, he loves us anyway. Chances are we're no less precious in God's eyes than the neighbor we envy or the co-worker who seems to have it all. So, who are we fooling?

Perhaps the best policy is to take courage and stop worrying about what everyone else is doing. Let's stand up and bravely show our true "reality" selves to the world. Now, that would make God smile!

Your unfailing love, O Lord,
is as vast as the heavens;
your faithfulness reaches beyond the clouds.
How precious is your unfailing love, O God!
Psalm 36:5,7a (NLT)

Be Still
for a
Silent Moment with God

Digging Deeper

Describe someone you know who puts on a good face, but has serious issues.

In what ways can you see yourself doing the same thing?

How could you have a more realistic view of yourself and your friend?

Prayer for Today

Why do I judge myself so harshly when others seem to have everything that I lack? Let me understand them as they really are, struggles and all. Help me realize, God, that you don't expect me to have it all together. All I really need is you! Amen.

Your Thoughts

∾

Why doesn't God simply swoop down
and fix everything that's wrong?

Mr. Fix-It

"...For I know the plans I have for you," says the LORD.
"They are plans for good and not for disaster,
to give you a future and a hope."
Jeremiah 29:11 (NLT)

"I'm so frustrated! Nothing's going right and my life is totally messed up. Why can't Jesus come down, wave his hands, and fix all my problems? I could really go for a little help right now!"

Have you ever felt like this? It's hard to understand why God doesn't simply swoop down and correct everything that has gone wrong. After all, he loves us—right? Why can't life be the way we want it?

That sounds lovely. But if Jesus constantly fixed every detail of our lives, we would be robbed of a spiritual opportunity. In a way, these trials offer us a chance to open our hearts to God and draw closer to him.

God allows us to make our own choices. Sometimes we mess up and are hurt by our own actions. Sometimes other people cause us pain through their shortcomings. But no matter who made the hurtful choice, a journey of healing looms ahead. If this struggle were taken away, we might be shallow creatures indeed.

There is another remedy for life's challenges. Instead of complaining about difficult situations, we can listen for God's voice. Is he whispering words of encouragement and hope? Is he asking us to forgive ourselves and others?

As we begin to hear, we discover that God has a greater purpose in our trials than we thought. So let's settle down, find a comfy spot, and have a long chat with God.

I will instruct you and teach you
in the way you should go;
I will counsel you with my loving eye on you.
Psalm 32:8 (NIV)

Be Still
for a
Silent Moment with God

Digging Deeper

When do you yearn for a "fix-it" solution to your problems?

What would be a better way to deal with your frustration?

What purpose do you think God has in mind for your life and healing?

Prayer for Today

Sometimes I feel so exasperated. Why do I have so many problems, God? I just want you to fix everything for me right now! I know, I know. That really wouldn't be best for me. Help me to relax and listen to your voice as we walk a healing path together. Amen.

Your Thoughts

৵

As many times as we stray from God,
he delights in opening his arms again.

The Caged Bird Returns

Give all your worries and cares to God,
for he cares about you.
1 Peter 5:7 (NLT)

Have you read the famous poem, "I Know Why the Caged Bird Sings," by Maya Angelou? One bird is free, and the other is caged. Unlike the free bird, the caged bird is imprisoned. So he sings of his longing to escape.

Who wouldn't want to be free? It's a normal and natural desire—especially for humans. But liberty doesn't always bring the desired results. Some captive birds, when set free, will return to what is most familiar—even to another cage and the loss of freedom.

This is commonly true when dealing with an unhealthy situation. Try as she might to fly away toward a new life, an abused woman is often drawn back into her harmful setting.

Perhaps it is the only environment she has known, and it's hard to comprehend a different life. So she returns to what feels safe, but really isn't.

The spiritual life operates in much the same way. We long to be free of old habits and sins, to journey forward with Christ. But the past beckons us, and before we know it, we're right back where we started.

What can we do? On average, people return to their old habits seven times before cutting ties. But each instance of escape gets a little easier as we inch away, firmly grasping God's hand.

The trick is to not become discouraged. As many times as we stray away from God, he delights in opening his arms again.

Let me hear of your
unfailing love each morning,
for I am trusting you.
Show me where to walk,
for I give myself to you.
Psalm 143:8 (NLT)

Be Still
for a
Silent Moment with God

Digging Deeper

In what ways are you caged and can't seem to get free?

Why do you remain there?

How could you hold God's hand as you inch toward freedom?

Prayer for Today

With you there is freedom every day. But I often fail to reach out and grasp it. Something holds me back and I stay chained to my difficulties. Help me to grow past what hinders me. Take my hand, God, and lead me, however haltingly, to your eternal freedom and love. Amen.

Your Thoughts

⋙

When we cling tightly to problems and issues,
it's hard for God to help us.

Monkey Business

"…This is my command—
be strong and courageous!
Do not be afraid or discouraged.
For the LORD your God
is with you wherever you go."
Joshua 1:9 (NLT)

A popular parable describes an ancient method for catching monkeys. All the hunter needed was a coconut with a hole drilled in one end. A bit of cooked rice or sweet treat was inserted through the opening. Then he anchored the coconut to a tree for the monkeys to find.

When a monkey wandered over and discovered the coconut, he would reach inside to grab the food. But then his hand was too full to remove it from the hole. Because he refused to let go of the treat, the monkey's arm was stuck and he was caught.

Is there a parallel in our spiritual lives? A lot of us have problems we can't seem to shake. Perhaps we've been hurt in the past. Or maybe we're struggling with a current situation. However much we'd like to shed these troubles, something keeps pulling us back in. Why does it keep happening?

Perhaps there is something attractive about holding onto problems. Why wouldn't the monkey give up the food? Is there some internal reward for staying trapped? Or do we simply hope our situation will improve but it never does?

When we cling tightly to these problems and issues, it's hard for God to help us. We need to release the food and pull our hands out of the coconut. It's time to let go.

The LORD hears his people
when they call to him for help.
He rescues them from all their troubles.
Psalm 34:17 (NLT)

Be Still
for a
Silent Moment with God

Digging Deeper

What problems or situations are you holding onto?

Is there a reason you can't let go? What is it?

How can you let God help?

Prayer for Today

I'm stuck! I need help. I'm like a monkey that can't get free. Help me to loosen my grip on my troubles, God. Show me that I don't need to stay like this, that there's a pathway out. Gently take my hand and lead me on your new road of freedom and love. Amen.

Your Thoughts

❦

As we forge a new path, companions will spring up along the way to walk with us.

When You Can't Go Home

He came to his own people,
And even they rejected him.
John 1:11 (NLT)

Can we always go home? Will our family and friends receive us, no matter how we've changed or grown over the years? We like to think so. But reality may be a stark contrast to the happy picture we envision.

Transformation is a perplexing topic. We can embark on a voyage of personal growth and healing that enlightens our inner world. We can walk through a deep spiritual journey that brings us closer to God. We're different now. But for those closest to us, this may present a challenge.

When a loved one changes significantly, relationships can be altered. Old ways of connecting don't work anymore, causing relatives and friends to feel uncomfortable.

They don't know how to interact and may even run from the relationship.

I wonder what happened to the people Jesus healed. Many had been rejected and outcast for years. After the miracles, did their communities adjust and accept them back? I'm guessing many did not. Old ways of relating are hard to change. Perhaps those who were rejected were able to find love and support elsewhere.

Spiritual growth and healing transform us, and yet a time may come when a trusted circle of support shuts us out. So it's a comfort to know we're not alone in this struggle. Even Jesus was rejected, but that didn't stop him.

However painful it is to forge a new path, companions will spring up along the way to walk with us. God will see to it!

Truly my soul finds rest in God;
my salvation comes from him.
Truly he is my rock and my salvation;
he is my fortress, I will never be shaken.
Psalm 62:1–2 (NIV)

Be Still
for a
Silent Moment with God

Digging Deeper

Do you sometimes feel rejected? In what ways could it be because you've changed?

What ways have you found to cope with this?

Have personal change and spiritual growth been worth the challenge? How?

Prayer for Today

I know Jesus faced rejection and pain. I have too. Sometimes it's hard to understand why a once supportive community would turn away from me as I grow. Help me to overcome my hurt feelings, God. Walk with me as we find new companions for the journey. I know you'll be with me forever. Amen.

Your Thoughts

ॐ

Sometimes pruning is necessary to
make room for wonderful new possibilities.

Pulled Away

…being confident of this, that
he who began a good work in you
will carry it on to completion
until the day of Christ Jesus.
Philippians 1:6 (NIV)

Have you ever worked really hard on a task? Or tried to be an extra special Christian friend to someone? Then, suddenly the rug is pulled out from under you. Boom! It's all gone terribly wrong, you're hurting and you don't know why.

How can we find God in the midst of such circumstances? Persevering in the Christian life is a challenge when precious people and situations are taken from us. We do the best we can, and yet sorrow drains our energy. Merely carrying out daily tasks requires a monumental effort. A bulldozer experience is not easily overcome.

But there is a hidden truth we may have forgotten: God knows more than we do. We can rest in the wisdom that he sees and understands everything. God knows the events that feel so hurtful now may yield benefits in the long run.

Years ago, in a previous job, a boss treated me unfairly. I was deeply hurt. It bothered me for years. Eventually, I realized I could not have accomplished other goals in my life—endeavors that helped a great many people—if I had stayed with that company. God, in his wisdom, removed me and set me on the path he wanted.

It hurts to be pulled away from something we love and enjoy. But sometimes pruning is necessary to make room for wonderful new possibilities. Hard as it can be to realize, God is preparing us for a bright future, even in the most painful times. No matter what seems to be falling apart, his presence is always there to comfort us.

I was pushed back and about to fall,
but the Lord helped me.
The Lord is my strength and my defense;
he has become my salvation.
Psalm 118:13–14 (NIV)

Be Still
for a
Silent Moment with God

Digging Deeper

When has a person or situation been pulled away from you?

Did anything good come from the experience? What?

Where do you see God's hand working on your behalf?

Prayer for Today

So many difficult trials have overwhelmed me. Often I have felt desolate and alone. But time has passed, and now I can see new possibilities that weren't there before. Help me understand what you are doing in my life, God. Lead me in the way you want me to go. Amen.

Your Thoughts

≫

God gives us the courage to turn around,
face our problems, and move ahead.

At the End of the Day

Don't be afraid, for I am with you.
Don't be discouraged, for I am your God.
I will strengthen you and help you.
I will hold you up with my victorious right hand.
Isaiah 41:10 (NLT)

People have lots of problems. There are lots of ways to fix these problems, which often translate into lots of ways to hide from them. Not surprisingly, most of these solutions aren't very effective, and so we end up with…lots of problems.

Some of us try to conceal our issues through drinking alcohol. Others do it by overworking. Many use status and achievement. Some overeat. It is impossible to count all the ingenious ways we've created to hide from troubles and pain. But each one is still merely a cover-up.

At the end of the day, where are we? If we've spent our time hiding, avoiding, and covering, won't we be in the same position as when we started? But if we could only find a real cure, the end of the day would bring hope and peace.

Much of our pain is either physical or emotional. Yet there is often a significant component that requires a spiritual resolution. When we finally admit our need to stop running and face the issues squarely, we'll need help—divine help.

Perhaps your issue requires forgiveness. Perhaps it calls for faith. Whatever the solution, God will gladly provide the courage to turn around, face the problem, and finally move ahead.

Don't forget—God cares! According to the prophet Isaiah, he has even written your name on the palm of his hand. Try basking in this love.

Wait patiently for the LORD.
Be brave and courageous.
Yes, wait patiently for the LORD.
Psalm 27:14 (NLT)

Be Still
for a
Silent Moment with God

Digging Deeper

Where are you at the end of your day?

Where do you want to be?

How can God help you get there?

Prayer for Today

Help me to stop running and hiding, God. I've devised so many ingenious ways to ignore my problems that I can hardly keep track of them. But at the end of the day I'm still stuck and going nowhere. Gently guide me into a life of joy with you. Amen.

Your Thoughts

૭ે

There's nothing like pain
to spur us on to spiritual change.

Overboard

"…Though the mountains be shaken
and the hills be removed,
yet my unfailing love for you will not be shaken
nor my covenant of peace be removed,"
says the LORD, who has compassion on you.
Isaiah 54:10 (NIV)

What feels better: rowing your boat in clear, calm water with loved ones on a refreshing outing? Or being thrown off the boat, all alone, into the cold, choppy sea with no rescue in sight? Hmm—I'll bet you would choose number one. Who wouldn't?

When we have equilibrium in our lives, all is well. The road is smooth. We feel contented and at peace. Our creative and productive capacities seem endless. When our lives are in balance, we drink in the sweet essence of God's peace.

But when chaos strikes, suddenly we're disoriented, scared, and lost. It doesn't matter whether we stood up in the boat and capsized it ourselves, or somebody pushed us overboard. Either way, we're out of kilter and off center. Our world has gone awry.

Losing our sense of stability can be an agonizing experience. But there's nothing like pain to spur us on to spiritual change. No longer can we remain enveloped in our cushy cocoons. When something—or someone—forces the issue, we're thrown headlong into an unexpected transformation.

My little rowboat has been rocked several times over the years. The loss of equilibrium has been painfully unsettling. But, in looking back, my spiritual path would be shallow without it. Perhaps you have made the same observation in your own life.

Falling overboard just feels lousy. However, from a Christian perspective, it's an okay place to be. After all, it gives us room for growth and the incentive to reach up and grab God's hand.

The LORD is close to the brokenhearted
and saves those who are crushed in spirit.
Psalm 34:18 (NIV)

Be Still
for a
Silent Moment with God

Digging Deeper

When have you lost your spiritual or emotional equilibrium?

What was the most effective way to get yourself back on an even keel?

Where was God in your experience?

Prayer for Today

Sometimes I feel like I've lost my way. Everything is unbalanced, and nothing makes sense. It's a bewildering time of radical change. Pull me out of the water, God, and set my boat upright again. Then we'll climb aboard and sail together in a new direction, full of love and laughter. Amen.

Your Thoughts

A Time to Change

❦

It can be hard to let go of
painful situations and bad habits.

Dumpster Diving

Therefore, if anyone is in Christ,
the new creation has come;
The old has gone, the new is here.
2 Corinthians 5:17 (NIV)

Do you ever wake up in the middle of the night and can't get back to sleep? It's so frustrating! But sometimes, in that half-awake, half-asleep state, weird pictures flash in our minds that yield surprising insights.

As I lay sleepless one night, I saw my arm crammed up to my shoulder into one of those fast food trash cans. You've seen them—big, square, plastic bins where customers toss their garbage on the way out of the restaurant.

In my odd midnight vision, I was dragging that garbage can everywhere. For some reason, I didn't even try to break free. Then God asked, "Why don't you just pull your arm out?" What a novel idea!

It's hard for many of us to let go of painful situations and bad habits. Why is that? Do we believe we aren't good enough to break free? Perhaps we feel we're somehow to blame for the difficulties that plague us. We may even hold onto the status quo because it's the only life we know.

How many of us carry a load of garbage around for years, rather than accepting God's healing? And how many of us are blind to the restorative power of forgiveness—both for ourselves and others? Could today be the day we pull our arms out of the trash bins? It's time to park that big, black box of pain on the curb. If the choice is God's way or trash, let's choose God!

He lifted me out of the pit of despair,
out of the mud and the mire.
He set my feet on solid ground
and steadied me as I walked along.
Psalm 40:2 (NLT)

Be Still
for a
Silent Moment with God

Digging Deeper

What keeps you tied to old garbage?

How can you kick the dumpster habit?

Where does God figure into your plan?

Prayer for Today

I'm stuck, and I need help! I can't seem to let go of all the hurtful baggage in my life. I know you don't create junk, God, but why is it so hard for me to believe that? I want to pull away from negative influence and embrace your love. Amen.

Your Thoughts

❧

The flowers of yesterday are
contained in the buds of tomorrow.

Last Year's Crops

Forgetting what is behind
and straining toward what is ahead,
I press on toward the goal to win the prize
for which God has called me heavenward
in Christ Jesus.
Philippians 3:13b–14 (NIV)

How much energy have you spent in the past year thinking about situations in your life that went awry? Perhaps a romantic relationship didn't work out. Or maybe there was a problem at work or with a relative. Whether the situation is miniscule or huge, we dash back and forth in our minds, hoping for a different outcome—or at least an explanation.

Continuing to fret about problems we can't fix is like watering last year's crops over and over. We're obsessed. We lose our focus. We connect our hoses and pour gallons of water onto old, wilted flowers, hoping they will magically return to life.

Is this really what Jesus wants for us? The season for these plants has passed. New opportunities are on the horizon. Fresh challenges are waiting to be met. But our fields are crowded with droopy plants that will never bloom again. How will we make room for tender little buds, eager to grow?

It's time to plow under those old crops. Shattered dreams of the past won't yield new fruit. But they can provide nourishment to the soil as we plant and cultivate a fresh crop of hopes and aspirations. All is not lost. The flowers of yesterday will be contained in the buds of tomorrow. In this new season, let's take God's hand and cultivate a lovely new garden.

When doubts filled my mind,
your comfort gave me
renewed hope and cheer.
Psalm 94:19 (NLT)

Be Still
for a
Silent Moment with God

Digging Deeper

What past situations occupy your thoughts?

What are you missing out on by continuing to ruminate on them?

How might God help you let go and move ahead?

Prayer for Today

Help! I keep looking back at all those drooping and wilted plants from long ago. But, God, you have glorious fields of fresh flowers just waiting for me to romp through them. Hold tightly to my hand and show me how to leave the past behind. Let us stroll through lush and fragrant gardens together. Amen.

Your Thoughts

❦

Allow a gentle breeze to caress your face.
Could the Holy Spirit be speaking to you?

Open a Window

So we don't look at the troubles we can see now;
rather, we fix our gaze on things that cannot be seen.
For the things we see now will soon be gone,
but the things we cannot see will last forever.
2 Corinthians 4:18 (NLT)

Feeling stuck? Sometimes all we need is a new perspective. *Dead Poets Society* is a film about learning to think differently. When a group of schoolboys needed a fresh outlook, their teacher encouraged them to stand on top of their desks to see life from another angle.

This actually works. Years ago, when I was remodeling my house, I wanted to add another bathroom. But try as I might, I couldn't figure out where to put it.

So I climbed up on a table and stood there for a bit. Gradually, an idea crystallized in my mind for a unique placement of the bathroom. If I hadn't changed my perspective, I doubt such a creative solution would have emerged.

If standing on furniture is a little too dramatic for you, but you still need a new outlook on life, try opening a window. Watch the sun beams shine through. Allow a gentle breeze to part the curtains and caress your face. Could the Holy Spirit be speaking to you?

Stay very still. Listen as God whispers new ideas and solutions. As you gaze through the window, your viewpoint can change. Outside that one small, stuffy room, a landscape brimming with possibilities could emerge just for you!

You will show me the way of life,
granting me the joy of your presence
and the pleasures of living with you forever.
Psalm 16:11 (NLT)

Be Still
for a
Silent Moment with God

Digging Deeper

Do you feel stuck? What is the situation?

How can you facilitate a change of perspective?

Where do you see God in this?

Prayer for Today

Help, I feel trapped! No matter what I do, the same thoughts keep swirling around my mind. I can't seem to break free and move forward with my life. Show me a new perspective, God, a different way. Open a window and fill my soul with fresh ideas for change. Amen.

Your Thoughts

≫

God, your steady hand on my shoulder
gives me strength to go on.

Turning Corners

"…Do not be afraid or discouraged,
for the LORD will personally go ahead of you.
He will be with you;
he will neither fail you nor abandon you."
Deuteronomy 31:8 (NLT)

Have you ever walked a labyrinth? It's an ancient Christian tradition dating from the twelfth century. Many cathedrals in Europe have them. A labyrinth is like a maze, except you can't get lost. It's filled with turns and bends with only one way in and one way out. There is usually a space in the center for prayer. Sounds a bit like life, doesn't it?

Walking a labyrinth is a reflective experience. Strolling through the curves on your way to the center, you can leave behind the worries of the day and meet God unfettered. After a time of silent prayer in the middle, you can journey back to the start and take up your life again with renewed energy and clarity.

Once I walked a labyrinth with some friends, and we compared notes afterward. One woman said she struggled with all the twists and turns. Her life was full of difficult transitions at that time.

Approaching a curve in life and knowing we must turn is tough. Sometimes, agonizing circumstances are thrust upon us. Other times we gladly choose our course, yet seem inexplicably unable to move our feet around the corner.

But one benefit of a labyrinth is that we're never alone. Other people are on the path too. Some join their lives with ours; others just give a friendly smile or word of encouragement. Our best travel companion, Jesus, is there too—waiting right around the bend, beckoning us forward. Can you see him?

Show me the right path, O LORD;
point out the right road for me to follow.
Psalm 25:4 (NLT)

Be Still
for a
Silent Moment with God

Digging Deeper

What twists and turns are you facing now?

Do you see ways to help you cope with change? What are they?

Where do you see Jesus along your path?

Prayer for Today

How I wish my path in life could be simple and straight. But that never seems to happen. I'm caught up in so many changing circumstances and painful situations. Be with me, God, as I navigate through it all. Your steady hand on my shoulder gives me strength to go on. Amen.

Your Thoughts

It would be lovely to live in our
comfort zone all the time. But we can't.

In the Zone

...let God transform you into a new person
by changing the way you think.
Then you will learn to know God's will for you...
Romans 12:2 *(NLT)*

Where do you feel most comfortable? I'm not talking about a favorite neighborhood café. What part of your being beckons you most often? Do you enjoy talking or listening? Reaching out to others or silently contemplating life? Being on the move, or sitting by a peaceful mountain stream?

We each have our own comfort zone. And wouldn't it be lovely to live there all the time? But we can't. Demands on our time, challenging circumstances, and life in general often force us to shift from the places we love best.

Difficult as it is, expanding our zone can have real benefits for us. Too often we tend to hide in the place that feels safe, restricting our healing and growth. But along the path to wholeness, we learn to flex emotional muscles that may not have been used for years.

For example, perhaps you have felt uncomfortable expressing yourself, fearful of the consequences. But as you make progress, your voice becomes sure and steady. Little by little, our comfort zones are expanded and redefined. We no longer live in one little isolated corner of our existence.

Having a comfort zone is, well, comforting! And yet, as our souls are healed and strengthened, we come to appreciate the advantages of a rich and varied spiritual life. Rather than operate on one tiny edge of the zone, why not live in balance? When we honor all sides of our being, God smiles.

The Lord is my light and my salvation—
whom shall I fear?
The Lord is the stronghold of my life—
of whom shall I be afraid?
Psalm 27:1 (NIV)

Be Still
for a
Silent Moment with God

Digging Deeper

Where is your favorite comfort zone?

How could you expand it?

What balance do you think God wants for your life?

Prayer for Today

How I love my comfort zone. It's my secret hideaway where I can disappear, so no one can see my pain. But I know that's not good for me. Help me to heal, God, and to expand my world. I want to move beyond the zone and live in balance with you. Amen.

Your Thoughts

୬

When we take off our masks,
we can begin to know God's healing grace.

Behind the Mask

Jesus turned and saw her.
"Take heart, daughter," he said,
"your faith has healed you."
And the woman was healed at that moment.
Matthew 9:22 (NIV)

Years ago, I heard a man say, "God can't heal a façade." He went on to remark that many of us walk around attached to a projector, making sure everyone sees only what we want them to see.

Is it wrong to present a favorable image? Not really. Putting our best foot forward is fine. Who wouldn't want to display their most admirable traits? But when the foot we're parading on is dishonest—when we pretend to be someone we're not—that's a problem.

There's also that nagging little question about Jesus. Would he actually be taken in by a façade? Not hardly. To paraphrase a quote attributed to Abraham Lincoln, "You can fool some of the people all of the time and all of the people some of the time..." but you can't fool Jesus any of the time!

We need to take off our masks, but the task feels daunting. Are we ashamed of who we really are? We may think we're not good enough and won't be accepted. Or perhaps we actually believe those enticing lies flickering across our personal movie screens and don't want to give them up.

How can we be more honest and transparent? As we slowly and carefully begin to reveal our true selves, do we dare to believe we'll be accepted? We may not be. But even if some reject us, it's still better to face the world honestly. When we take off our masks, we can begin to know God's healing grace.

May the words of my mouth
and the meditation of my heart
be pleasing to you,
O LORD, my rock and my redeemer.
Psalm 19:14 (NLT)

Be Still
for a
Silent Moment with God

Digging Deeper

Describe your favorite mask.

What do you gain by continuing to wear that mask?

What are some ways that God could help you remove it?

Prayer for Today

I don't want to try to fool you or anyone else, God. I'm just afraid to let people see who I really am. Please help me take off my mask. I trust you to protect me, even if others are hurtful and rejecting. Be with me as I reveal my true face. Amen.

Your Thoughts

୬

Pursuing an unworkable situation
could distract us from our true calling.

Missing the Boat

And we know that in all things
God works for the good of those who love him,
who have been called according to his purpose.
Romans 8:28 (NIV)

Some things just don't work out. The loss could have been a relationship, a job, or other opportunity. Whatever the details, it was important, and you had your heart set on it. But it's not going to materialize. So, what happens now?

It's easy to spiritualize the situation and believe God will eventually work everything out for our happiness. Why wouldn't he? After all, we rationalize we're his children and he must want the best for us. Shouldn't that include what we think is the best?

But that doesn't always happen. Sometimes we're called to let go. It's agonizing to loosen our grip on a dream we've treasured for a long time. We leave a trail of fingernail marks as we're dragged away from our cherished hope.

Could it be that God has a new direction in mind? When our plan feels hopelessly stalled, perhaps it's best to gracefully set it aside. Trying to force something that isn't meant to be doesn't sound like a wise strategy.

Probably the most compelling reason to let go is that pursuing an unworkable situation could distract us from our true calling. How sad to spend precious time in frustration and delay, when God has a wonderful plan just for us.

Maybe it's time to let go of one dream and set out in a new direction. We don't want to miss the boat with God. So climb aboard and trust him for a great adventure!

The LORD will work out
his plans for my life—
for your faithful love,
O LORD, endures forever.
Psalm 138:8a (NLT)

Be Still
for a
Silent Moment with God

Digging Deeper

What are you holding onto?

If you weren't focused on that situation, what would you be doing?

How can you trust God to help you make that change?

Prayer for Today

Am I missing the boat with you, God? I have so many hopes and dreams that never seem to become reality. Is it because, however lovely they are, you have better ideas? Lead me over to your boat and help me climb in. We'll sail toward the horizon, discovering everything you've planned for me. Amen.

Your Thoughts

ॐ

By staying boxed in,
we miss out on God's greater plans for us.

REFLECTION 18

Breaking Free

"You are truly my disciples
if you remain faithful to my teachings.
And you will know the truth,
and the truth will set you free."
John 8:31a–32 (NLT)

Do you ever feel boxed in? Perhaps others want you to act
a certain way, look a certain way, or even "be" a certain
way. But that isn't what you would choose. And you have a
sneaking suspicion it's not what God wants for you either.

What are the tell-tale signs that something's not quite
right? You might feel stuck in a career that was someone
else's idea. Or perhaps a confining relationship is starting to
squeeze you. Even the smallest details of life can add to the
sense that you're trapped. No matter how you try to adjust,
there's an uneasy feeling in your soul.

Where's the answer? Check in with God and quietly listen for his guidance. Prayerful reflection is the key step in beginning this journey.

Next we face the hard work of change. Taking stock of our lives isn't easy. It can take a long time to understand your situation, how you got there, and ways to break free. Following through with a plan of action requires courage and commitment.

The cost of freedom remains a difficult challenge. Separating from the expectations of others can cause hard feelings and rifts in relationships. But the status quo has a price too. By staying "boxed in" we miss out on God's greater plans for us. Is that a price we're willing to pay?

When hard pressed, I cried to the LORD;
he brought me into a spacious place.
Psalm 118:5 (NIV)

Be Still
for a
Silent Moment with God

Digging Deeper

In what ways do you feel boxed in by the expectations of others?

What choices can you make to change that feeling?

What do you suppose God's plans are for you in this situation?

Prayer for Today

You know I'm yours, God. But sometimes other people think I'm theirs too, and it's hard for me to tell what's right. I want to stand in your energy and strength as I become the person you have designed me to be. Help me break free and be solely yours! Amen.

Your Thoughts

❧

Are we so obsessed with our issues that
we fail to notice the struggles of others?

Who's Watching

You became imitators of us and of the LORD,
for you welcomed the message
in the midst of severe suffering
with the joy given by the Holy Spirit.
1 Thessalonians 1:6 (NIV)

Years ago I saw a film about Franklin Roosevelt, former President of the United States. He was stricken with polio as a young man and coped with disability for the rest of his life.

The movie focused on his early struggles with the disease, including several visits to a health spa. Because his political aspirations were in shambles, he was consumed by anger and self-pity.

This blinded him to the plight of other polio patients at the spa. But as his eyes were gradually opened, his compassion for his fellow suffers began to grow. In time, his ability to overcome his infirmities proved an inspiration to all.

I can relate to Roosevelt's experience. As a community leader and domestic violence survivor, I was asked to speak to a group of women struggling with this difficult issue. After my short, simple speech, I was astonished to see the audience jump to its feet in applause. Later, the women formed a long line to personally tell me their stories.

I didn't realize the impact a common experience could have on those who faced dangerous situations. Somehow, my story gave them hope and the courage to heal and move forward.

So it is with our spiritual lives. How often do we obsess over our own issues and fail to notice the similar struggles of someone else? If we focus instead on reflecting Christ to others, real healing begins—for all of us.

My life is an example to many,
because you have been my strength and protection.
Psalm 71:7 (NLT)

Be Still
for a
Silent Moment with God

Digging Deeper

Could you be an example to others without even knowing it? How?

In what ways are you able to help your fellow sufferers?

How do you sense God's presence in this effort?

Prayer for Today

I get so caught up in my own problems that often I don't see anyone else's suffering. Sometimes my troubles are all I can bear. God, help me consider others who walk similar paths. They need my compassion and attention too. May I always be the example you want me to be. Amen.

Your Thoughts

⚘

It takes courage to walk in a new level of trust,
but God promises to be with us.

Moving In

You will be rewarded for this;
your hope will not be disappointed.
Proverbs 23:18 (NLT)

It's tough to leave the past behind. Our old paradigms have great influence, no matter what's happening to us now. It's like we've placed colored lenses over our eyes and can't see the world as it really is.

When we don't accurately perceive a situation, it's hard to respond well to the challenges that continually confront us. It's as if we're afraid of ghosts long dead, reacting to circumstances that are no longer present.

This way of viewing the world hurts us and others. The issues driving our lives are clouded in the past, inflicting needless pain and fueling misunderstanding and bewilderment in those we love.

A friend of mine struggled greatly with old issues. Because of a hurtful past, he hesitated to fully commit to life. The distorted lens of his early life hindered him. Each time he acquired a new home, he never quite moved in, always leaving his tie rack packed away. One day, he finally made a giant leap forward. He hung the tie rack in his closet and emotionally moved on with life.

God doesn't want us to be immobilized. The framework of our youth isn't necessarily the one he holds before us today. We've grown. Much experience has enriched our lives, and our souls are not the same anymore.

It takes courage to remove our distorted lenses and walk in a new level of trust, but God promises to be with us. Is it time to put those glasses away and move ahead?

Be strong and take heart,
all you who hope in the LORD.
Psalm 31:24 (NIV)

Be Still
for a
Silent Moment with God

Digging Deeper

In what ways may you be tied to an old paradigm?

How might God be calling you to a new way of trusting him?

What small changes could you make in your life today?

Prayer for Today

Why is it so hard for me to see reality? Sometimes I feel trapped in the past and can't get out. But that just causes more and more pain. God, help me take off these distorted glasses. Lend me your hand as I discover new vision, a better way of living. Amen.

Your Thoughts

A Time with Jesus

಄

Our feelings about ourselves often
get in the way of our relationship with God.

The Porch Swing

I—yes, I alone—will
blot out your sins for my own sake
and will never think of them again.
Isaiah 43:25 *(NLT)*

It's so easy to get bogged down by our mistakes. No matter how hard we try, we can't do everything perfectly. A blunder here, an error of judgment there, and pretty soon our record is full of transgressions that we can never erase. It sometimes seems like God himself will never overlook our past.

Imagine you are sitting in an old, white porch swing overlooking a lovely garden. Jesus walks by and asks if he can join you. Since the swing will easily hold two, you beckon him to sit with you.

But there's a problem. A big, heavy garbage bag sits right in the middle, between you and Jesus. It's full of everything you've ever done wrong. Try as you might, you just can't get comfortable because the bag is squashing you.

Jesus notices and says kindly, "Let me take care of this." He hoists the bag onto his shoulder and carries it behind the house, where he tosses it into an incinerator. Soon the contents of the bag are obliterated. He returns and the two of you sit close and slowly swing as the tranquil afternoon passes into evening.

Often our feelings about ourselves and our problems get in the way of our relationship with God. But it doesn't have to be that way. Jesus is ready and willing to help. So call him!

For as high as the heavens are above the earth,
so great is his love for those who fear him;
as far as the east is from the west,
so far has he removed our transgressions from us.
Psalm 103:11–12 (NIV)

Be Still
for a
Silent Moment with God

Digging Deeper

What is separating you from God today?

In what ways could Jesus help?

How could removing the "garbage" affect your life?

Prayer for Today

I feel so weighed down by all that's happened in my life. It seems like nothing will ever get better. But, God, I know you don't want the two of us to be separated. Please help me to put everything behind me. Then let's sit together and happily swing for the rest of the day and into eternity. Amen!

Your Thoughts

℘

God specially designed each one of us.
We're exactly what he wants!

Peeling Onions

So God created human beings in his own image.
In the image of God he created them;
male and female he created them.
Genesis 1:27 (NLT)

There's an old saying about peeling an onion. If you want to get to the root of a problem, keep peeling the layers back. Sooner or later, the heart of the issue will be revealed. Then simply keep that part of the onion and throw the peelings away.

But could this logic be flawed, at least from a spiritual point of view? As we peel away the layers, do we really expect to find something totally different? After all, in the end, we're still holding an onion.

We are who we are, down to our very core. Peeling away layers only takes off layers. It is a good idea to dig deeply and understand what's going on in our lives, but is it productive to throw away large chunks of ourselves? If we do, what's left?

We are made in God's image. Sometimes bits and pieces of us become tarnished and beaten up. Rather than peeling off the hurt parts and throwing them away, why not polish up the blemishes and buff out the dings? Is it possible to keep ourselves intact and gently repair the damage?

We are still ourselves underneath all those onion layers. God specially designed each one of us. We're exactly what he wants!

> *The LORD looks down from heaven*
> *and sees the whole human race.*
> *From his throne he observes*
> *all who live on the earth.*
> *He made their hearts,*
> *so he understands everything they do.*
> *Psalm 33:13–15 (NLT)*

Be Still
for a
Silent Moment with God

Digging Deeper

In what ways have you tried to solve problems by throwing away a piece of yourself?

Did that method seem helpful or hurtful?

How do you think God would handle the situation?

Prayer for Today

Sometimes I'm so eager to root out problems that I want to throw away big pieces of myself. But then I would be only a fragmented shadow. Every cell in my body is made in your image, God. Help me embrace this likeness and let it be reflected to everyone I meet. Amen.

Your Thoughts

❧

Let's allow God to reshape us
as we journey along with him.

Keeping the Clay

I went down to the potter's house,
and I saw him working at the wheel.
But the pot he was shaping from the clay
was marred in his hands;
so the potter formed it into another pot,
shaping it as seemed best to him.
Jeremiah 18:3–4 (NIV)

As we move through life, no one escapes pain and heartache. Perhaps we have caused some regrettable situations, or maybe difficulties have been imposed on us by others. Either way, we feel tainted. We wonder if God can ever use us to minister to others. But the undeniable answer is "Yes."

When a potter creates a vessel, he carefully forms it while turning the wheel. But sometimes it doesn't turn out quite right. So, what happens? The potter squashes the clay back down. Then, as the wheel continues to turn, he re-forms the pot into a new and better creation.

There is one thing the potter does not do. As he compresses the clay to begin again, he doesn't scoop out a bad chunk and throw it away. Instead, the pot is reshaped again, using all the clay.

Each of us struggles with painful experiences. As much as we don't like it, the struggle is part of who we are. We'd love to get rid of them and somehow start over again differently. But that's not how God works. He takes all our parts and pieces—good and bad—and forms us to be what he envisions.

Without painful experiences, our ministry to others would be less effective and empathetic. Rather than throw away pieces of our clay, let's allow God to reshape us as we journey along with him.

I praise you because
I am fearfully and wonderfully made;
your works are wonderful, I know that full well.
Psalm 139:14 (NIV)

Be Still
for a
Silent Moment with God

Digging Deeper

Is there a personal lump of clay that's holding you back? What is it?

How do you think God would reshape it?

What stops you from letting him touch it?

Prayer for Today

You know me. You know all about me, even the parts I would rather throw away. Help me, God, to accept the fragments that feel flawed. Take my lumps of clay and reshape them into the person you desire me to be, so I may serve and glorify you forever. Amen.

Your Thoughts

✑

When you face serious rejection,
reach for the hand that's always there.

Give Me Your Hand

"Do not let your hearts be troubled.
You believe in God; believe also in me."
John 14:1 (NIV)

Rejection—nobody likes it. The very word is painful. Maybe it represents the loss of a job. Maybe a relationship has been severed. Either way, it hurts. Sooner or later, it happens to everyone. But a few seem to be called to bear almost crushing burdens of rejection. Perhaps that's you.

Some are rejected for standing up to right a wrong. Others may have drawn a boundary against being badly treated. Many are rejected for their faith in Jesus Christ. And some don't even know why they are not accepted.

How can we handle rejection? There are many choices. We can rationalize it away, saying the rejecting party is wrong. We can go deeper and try to understand the psychological challenges of the hostile person. We can even decide that they must be right and conclude that we're worthless.

In the end, though, we have one special option. We can ask for a hand—the hand of Jesus. When we feel devastated and disparaged there really is no other place to turn. We can't change the situation, but with God's help, we can learn to move past it.

When you face serious rejection and feel like your life isn't worth much, reach for the hand that's always there. Together, you and Jesus can begin a journey toward peace.

> *The LORD directs the steps of the godly.*
> *He delights in every detail of their lives.*
> *Though they stumble, they will never fall,*
> *for the LORD holds them by the hand.*
> *Psalm 37:23–24 (NLT)*

Be Still
for a
Silent Moment with God

Digging Deeper

Are you facing serious rejection in your life? What is it?

What is your understanding of the situation?

How can you and God find a new direction to walk?

Prayer for Today

Rejection really hurts. Sometimes I don't even know why it happens. I've done the best I can, but painful relationships keep cropping up in my life. God, can you lead me away from all the hurt and into a land of peace? Let's walk together in a new direction. Amen.

Your Thoughts

If you've already taken your regrets to Jesus,
he's forgiven you. It's a done deal.

Tossing Pinecones

Forget the former things; do not dwell on the past.
See, I am doing a new thing!
Now it springs up; do you not perceive it?
Isaiah 43:18–19a (NIV)

Do you have past experiences you regret and wish they hadn't happened? Most of us do. Perhaps you made mistakes early in life. Maybe you are troubled by circumstances you can't change. Either way, you're struggling to find peace.

A trusted advisor once gave me the following two-step process to resolve these issues:

First, if you've already taken your regrets to Jesus, realize he has forgiven you. It may not feel that way, but from his perspective, it's a done deal. He's forgotten all about it. Try to rest in that truth, even if you don't sense his forgiveness yet.

Second, a symbolic action can often help resolve your feelings. For example, go outside and collect several pinecones (or acorns or other plentiful seed pods). Pick one for each situation you regret. They could represent people, places, or events.

Find a quiet area to sit. Pray over the first situation and let your emotions flow. Consider what your part was and what it wasn't. When you're finished, get up and walk a short distance. Then toss a pinecone as far as you can while gently and lovingly releasing that person or circumstance.

Repeat the process for all the pinecones you've collected. It may take some time, and you may feel exhausted afterward. But the troubling situations could soon become distant memories. Your sense of peace and wholeness returns as you walk forward with Jesus.

Finally, I confessed all my sins to you
and stopped trying to hide my guilt.
I said to myself,
"I will confess my rebellion to the LORD."
And you forgave me! All my guilt is gone.
Psalm 32:5 (NLT)

Be Still
for a
Silent Moment with God

Digging Deeper

Describe a situation you've confessed, but can't seem to get over.

What action could you take to put it in the past?

Where does Jesus fit in?

Prayer for Today

At times I'm overwhelmed by my failings and mistakes. Even when I take them to you, God, I still struggle. They don't go away. I know I'm forgiven, and you don't remember my misdeeds anymore. So, why do I? Take me by the hand and help me find peace again. Amen.

Your Thoughts

꙾

The trick is to keep moving forward
through the pain. Don't stop.

Let's Dance

"...He will take delight in you with gladness.
With his love, he will calm all your fears.
He will rejoice over you with joyful songs."
Zephaniah 3:17b (NLT)

A proverb from the African nation of Zimbabwe says, "If you can walk, you can dance. If you can talk, you can sing." What a captivating and enchanting outlook! I believe it also speaks about healing the wounds in our often fractured world.

Even when our spiritual lives are clipping along smoothly, it's not uncommon to hit a bump in the road. Something goes wrong in a relationship. An issue crops up at work. A sudden illness brings us down. When these challenges occur, we can take a cue from our African friends.

If we can just keep walking, even in the midst of troubles, eventually we'll be able to dance again. It may be painful and slow. Sometimes all we can do is put one foot in front of the other, heroically struggling to keep our balance. But that's all it takes.

Similarly, as you talk with God about the situation, your singing voice will be restored. The words may be hesitant and uncertain at first. You may sound more like a croaking frog than a songbird. But ultimately your voice will be healed, and your life filled with delightful melody.

The trick is to keep moving forward through the pain. Don't stop. Difficulties will come. But as your spiritual life strengthens, you'll find that Jesus never leaves. There he is, standing in the corner, playing a joyful tune as you dance around the room!

Sing to the LORD a new song.
Sing his praises in the assembly of the faithful.
Praise his name with dancing,
accompanied by tambourine and harp.
Psalm 149:1,3 (NLT)

Be Still
for a
Silent Moment with God

Digging Deeper

What is holding you back from singing and dancing?

How can you heal and recover your joyful spirit?

Where do you sense God's presence in your difficulties?

Prayer for Today

How I long to sing and dance again. I miss it so much! But right now dancing seems beyond my strength. I need your soothing touch, God. Gently show me the steps and teach me the words. Heal my heart and restore my joy as our voices join in a sparkling duet. Amen.

Your Thoughts

ço

God can be found at the core of every conflict,
reflecting whatever is good.

At the Core

God blesses those who work for peace,
for they will be called the children of God.
Matthew 5:9 (NLT)

How do you handle your emotions in an argument? Do you lash out? Do you withdraw to a safe place? Or do you simply endure the discomfort? Conflict is tough, and these days there's an abundance of it.

Disagreements are especially difficult when they touch sensitive issues. Perhaps we've been trying hard to heal and overcome life-long hurts. But when an argument starts, it's easy to be triggered into reactions that are less than helpful, both to us and others.

The list of "hot buttons" can feel endless. Not only do personal issues cause conflict, but theological and political questions often ignite a fire. It is possible, though, to handle these conversations in a loving and Christ-like manner.

Consider this novel idea: Jesus is not actually on either side. Instead, he is squarely in the center of each dispute. That doesn't mean he is in the wishy-washy, lukewarm middle. Rather, God can be found at the core of each conflict, reflecting whatever is good. Our job is to search for him and be with him, no matter how difficult.

To keep our eyes on God, it's important to listen and watch. However hard it may be, stand back and observe the issue as objectively as you can. Set aside your own thoughts, feelings, and biases. You'll see Jesus standing there, arms outstretched, waiting for you. When you stay close to him, a healing opportunity is opened for everyone involved.

The LORD is merciful and compassionate,
slow to get angry, and filled with unfailing love.
The LORD is good to everyone.
He showers compassion on all his creation.
Psalm 145:8–9 (NLT)

Be Still
for a
Silent Moment with God

Digging Deeper

What kind of arguments are you drawn into?

How could you pause and find where Jesus is standing?

In what ways would this help your healing process?

Prayer for Today

It's so hard to avoid being drawn into conflict! When I get into arguments, my old, unhealed self emerges, making a solution even harder to find. I'm looking to you, God, for help. Show me where you are in the midst of controversy, so I can join you and feel your healing touch. Amen.

Your Thoughts

∽

God looks past our smudges and smears
to see souls bathed in beauty.

Cut Off the Label

...put on the new self,
created to be like God
in true righteousness and holiness.
Ephesians 4:24 (NIV)

When we buy clothing, everything comes with a label—or maybe two or three. There's the manufacturer's label, the washing instructions, the price tag, and sometimes a sticky label detailing the size.

What about our personal labels? Do we use labels to tout our success, beauty, or all-around greatness? Do we wear our labels in full view, hoping those we meet will see them and be dutifully impressed? We want to look like we have it together and are making a splash in the world.

But inside, it's often a different story. How many of us secretly feel unattractive, inadequate, or unsure? How many wear an unseen label called unlovable, incompetent, or worthless? We hide these labels so no one will see. Unless a person really knows us well, it's impossible to guess what our labels actually say.

Thankfully, God doesn't see us that way. We were created for relationship with him. We've gotten a little tarnished from wear and tear. But God is able to look past the smudges and smears to see souls bathed in beauty.

Is it time to let God remove our scratchy labels? He'd like nothing better than to snip them off with his giant scissors. As the labels flutter to the ground, he will rejoice over us with gladness and singing.

> *I prayed to the Lord, and he answered me.*
> *He freed me from all my fears.*
> *Those who look to him for help will be radiant with joy;*
> *no shadow of shame will darken their faces.*
> *Psalm 34:4–5 (NLT)*

Be Still
for a
Silent Moment with God

Digging Deeper

What do your labels say?

Why do you hold on to them?

What would it take for you to let God clip them off?

Prayer for Today

You know me, God. You appreciate all my good and not-so-good points. But I'm afraid to let others see who I am inside. Sometimes I masquerade as someone I'm really not. Please clip off my labels and buff out my rough spots, so I can reflect you everywhere I go. Amen.

Your Thoughts

❧

We grow in spiritual depth as we
face and overcome the trials of life.

Picture This

And may you have the power to understand,
as all God's people should,
how wide, how long, how high,
and how deep his love is.
Ephesians 3:18 (NLT)

Imagine your life is encircled by a picture frame. How do you look? What are you doing? Who else is in the picture? Are they happy or sad? What about their body language? Sit for a moment and quietly visualize your portrait.

Each of our pictures will be unique. Some are fortunate to have enjoyable memories, loving families, and faithful friends throughout life. Some feel treasured and can visualize a frame filled with joyful expressions.

For many, however, the frame and its contents are not as pleasant. Perhaps you are encompassed by memories of difficult situations, broken relationships, and other events that have gone wrong. The faces in the frame bring only sadness. It's easy to become paralyzed, unable to move beyond a painful picture to wholeness and healing.

But there is good news. If you're not happy with your framed portrait, it's not too late to choose a different one. Consider featuring a wiser and more settled version of yourself. As you have faced and overcome the trials of life, you've grown in spiritual depth. In place of your lonely existence, a group of loving companions now surround you.

Now imagine your picture in a very special gilded frame. The Father and the Son tenderly encircle you as the Holy Spirit soars at the top like a dove. The old battered, splintered frame is gone. You are healed, surrounded by love, and eager to move forward in life.

Surely your goodness and love will follow me
all the days of my life,
and I will dwell in the house of the LORD forever.
Psalm 23:6 (NIV)

Be Still
for a
Silent Moment with God

Digging Deeper

What does the portrait inside your frame look like?

How could you fill the frame with a different picture?

Where do you see Jesus?

Prayer for Today

God, sometimes I'm so overwhelmed that I can't see you inside my frame. Perhaps you're lost in the complexity of the portrait. Step out of the background and take your rightful place. Encircle me with your love. And please bring Jesus and the Holy Spirit with you! Amen.

Your Thoughts

❧

Shackles are painful and constricting.
Is it time to break free?

Unshackled

*He has sent me to comfort the brokenhearted
and to proclaim that captives will be released
and prisoners will be freed.*
Isaiah 61:1b (NLT)

Is there an issue in your life that never seems to resolve? No matter what you do, it's still there, lurking under the surface, waiting to bubble up. Or perhaps it lives tucked away in a hidden corner of your mind. You may not realize it, but you're shackled.

There are many different kinds of shackles. You might be bound by handcuffs, unable to move your hands. Or your feet could be dragging a large, heavy ball. The worst kind is an iron piece clamped around your neck with chains restraining your arms and legs, resulting in total paralysis.

Being shackled feels horrible! The chains are clunky, noisy, constricting, and painful. There's no way to go where you want or do what you'd like. The best you can hope for is to slowly hobble along, struggling to keep your balance. The worst part is the suffering and shame. It's time to get free!

Picture this: Jesus appears, carrying the key to your shackles. After unlocking your chains, to your great surprise, they drop to the ground. Suddenly the pinching constraints are gone. You can move freely! As Jesus bends down to pick up the ugly shackles, he surprises you again. He suggests that you might want to transform the former restraints into something beautiful.

What on earth could that be? Could you turn them into a sculpture? Or maybe plant some flowers in them? There are many possibilities. What's most important is to remind yourself that life is different now. You're free. As you join God in an exciting new adventure, celebrate and praise him for giving you freedom.

"Lord, help!" they cried in their trouble,
and he saved them from their distress.
He led them from the darkness and deepest gloom;
he snapped their chains.
Psalm 107:13–14 (NLT)

Be Still
for a
Silent Moment with God

Digging Deeper

What is restraining you?

How can you be free?

What will you do with your newfound freedom?

Prayer for Today

I want to be free, but these shackles have bound me for as long as I can remember. They almost seem like a permanent part of my soul. God, please unlock my chains. As they tumble to the ground, let's dance freely together into the bright future you've planned for me. Amen.

Your Thoughts

A Time to Grow

❦

Sadness and regret build up over time
like barnacles on a boat.

Barnacles

...let us throw off everything that hinders
and the sin that so easily entangles.
And let us run with perseverance
the race marked out for us.
Hebrews 12:1 (NIV)

Consider this advice. It's common knowledge among sailors that a ship can't sail smoothly until the barnacles are scraped off. Have you ever seen a neglected boat covered with crusty sea creatures? It tries to move forward, but it's sluggish and difficult to steer.

Similarly, you can be hindered by events from the past. Perhaps unjust things have happened to you. Or possibly you did something you regret, but can't let go. Over time, sadness and regret build up like barnacles on a boat.

Whatever the issue, our lives can't get up to speed. We feel hampered in our efforts and unable to move forward. Excess baggage weighs us down and threatens to sink any progress we've made. Each time we try to plow through the waters, we end up exhausted and disheartened.

How do you suppose God feels about this? He may see our potential as sleek sailboats, able to gracefully traverse the waters. Or perhaps he built us to be sturdy little tugboats, chugging across the sea. And yet, in reality, our barnacles are dragging us farther away from our goals.

It's time to pull into dry dock and get a good cleaning. A little rest helps us to refocus. Then a gentle scraping chips away the residue of the past that has us mired in sludge. Finally, some polish will buff up our tired and worn exterior. Then we'll be smooth and swift as we set out on our next voyage with Jesus.

When they call on me, I will answer;
I will be with them in trouble.
I will rescue and honor them.
Psalm 91:15 (NLT)

Be Still
for a
Silent Moment with God

Digging Deeper

What are the barnacles on your personal boat?

What do you believe is God's vision for your life?

How could you scrape off the barnacles and be free?

Prayer for Today

These barnacles are killing me! Actually, that's not entirely true, but they sure do weigh me down. I know this isn't what you want for me, God. Cleanse me, so I can sail unburdened and free. You and I have many waters to explore as we cruise together forever. Amen.

Your Thoughts

၇

Can we accept that our pain
may never fully disappear?

Plowing Around the Stumps

*Though its roots have grown old in the earth
and its stump decays,
at the scent of water it will bud
and sprout again like a new seedling.*
Job 14:8–9 (NLT)

All of us have "tree stumps"—negative events or difficulties we couldn't overcome. Much as we want to remove them and smooth the ground, they remain deeply rooted. We continually stub our toes on those pesky lumps of wood!

We could try chopping them up. But what would we do with the roots? We may not have the strength to get rid of them by ourselves, especially when they run deep. It may be impossible to pull out all the hurt and pain they represent.

Perhaps there is another reason the stumps don't go away. The Apostle Paul struggled greatly with an apparent physical ailment. It was never healed or removed. Paul finally understood that God's grace was sufficient for him. Is that a lesson for us? Can we accept that our pain may never fully disappear?

Plowing around the stumps may be our best choice. But they needn't be an ugly souvenir of something we'd rather forget. How could we surround our stumps with beauty? There must be a way to transform them.

Perhaps we could plant a garden around them. We might conceal the rough edges with a patch of flowers or maybe a delightful shrub. Or perhaps young shoots from the stump might become the centerpiece of an exquisite new landscape. Whatever we create let it remind us that God doesn't judge us by our stumps. He sees only us, the children he loves!

But I am like an olive tree
flourishing in the house of God;
I trust in God's unfailing love for ever and ever.
Psalm 52:8 (NIV)

Be Still
for a
Silent Moment with God

Digging Deeper

Where are the stumps in your life?

What do you suppose is God's purpose in leaving them there?

If a stump never goes away, how can you transform it?

Prayer for Today

There are so many stumps in my garden. I can hardly walk without tripping over one of them. Help me, God, to overcome the pain they represent. Teach me to bring forth beauty from what was a painful and ugly memory. Let us build together a garden of peace and joy. Amen.

Your Thoughts

֍

When we've lost something precious,
its return is filled with sweetness.

The Donkey

Rejoice in our confident hope.
Be patient in trouble,
and keep on praying.
Romans 12:12 (NLT)

An old Turkish proverb says, "When God wants a pauper to be happy, he makes him lose his donkey. Then he lets him find it."

At first glance, it may seem strange that God would deliberately harm someone. After all, he's a loving God, not a tyrant. So perhaps the harm doesn't come from God, but rather the ups and downs of life itself. Things happen. The longer we live, the more opportunities arise for situations we'd rather not face.

What are some ways a donkey could represent something that matters to us? Perhaps it is a beloved relative or friend who is lost to us right now, through sickness or separation. Or maybe it's a treasured possession like a wedding ring rinsed down the sink.

The real key to the proverb is what happens to the man when his donkey is returned. Sometimes we don't realize how much we value something until it's gone. Its absence can leave an aching hole in your heart.

When we've lost something precious, its return is filled with sweetness. Even after years of waiting and hoping, our hearts rejoice and are filled with song. If we listen, we can hear God singing along with us in perfect harmony.

...weeping may stay the night,
but rejoicing comes in the morning.
Psalm 30:5b (NIV)

Be Still
for a
Silent Moment with God

Digging Deeper

Describe a "donkey" you once lost and then found.

Did this experience deepen your faith?

In what ways do you feel God was with you during this time?

Prayer for Today

I've had so many losses in my life. If they were donkeys, I'd have a whole herd by now! But through your gracious love, God, many have been restored to me. I thank you and praise you for all you've taught me. As we continue to walk together, help me to remember all my lovely donkeys. Amen.

Your Thoughts

❧

Can we learn to put sorrow behind us
and focus on the good?

Sucking Lemons

And whatever you do, whether in word or deed,
do it all in the name of the Lord Jesus,
giving thanks to God the Father through him.
Colossians 3:17 (NIV)

I once read a story about a minister who liked to visit nursing homes. He observed that the elderly people he met fell into one of two groups. After remembering their stories of a lifetime, they were either incredibly grateful or exceedingly bitter.

The grateful ones had often suffered much in their lives, perhaps even more than the bitter ones. But you'd never know it from talking with them. They were upbeat, interested in the world around them, and great listeners. Their faces were full of energy, empathy, and compassion.

The bitter people, on the other hand, spent so much time "sucking lemons" that they drove others away. They were hard to please, self-focused, and obsessed with their trials and difficulties. They weren't really interested in listening to anyone else. Instead, they demanded attention from all who came within earshot.

Each of us has had our share of difficulties in life. How are we doing at rising above them? Are we learning to put sorrow behind us and focus on the good? If so, we're like those elderly people who continue to positively impact others. If not, there's a good chance we'll end up being negative, cranky people that no one wants to be around.

According to the minister who visits the nursing homes, it's all about love. The grateful folks love and are loved. The bitter ones just suck lemons.

Give thanks to the LORD and proclaim his greatness.
Let the whole world know what he has done.
Sing to him; yes, sing his praises.
Tell everyone about his wonderful deeds.
Psalm 105:1–2 (NLT)

Be Still
for a
Silent Moment with God

Digging Deeper

What traits do you hope to have as an old person?

Do you ever find yourself sucking lemons? When?

What mid-course corrections can you make with God's help?

Prayer for Today

Sometimes I feel like I've fallen into a vat of lemon juice. I might even drown! God, please throw me a rope and pull me out. I want to be like Moses, whose face shone with God's spirit. Help me reflect the way of love to all I meet. Amen.

Your Thoughts

❧

Flowers, songs, and poems
can be enjoyed in the midst of every trial.

Making Peace with Reality

"But blessed are those who trust in the LORD
and have made the LORD their hope and confidence.
They are like trees planted along a riverbank,
with roots that reach deep into the water."
Jeremiah 17:7–8a (NLT)

Is there a persistently difficult situation in your life? No matter what you do—or don't do—it doesn't change. You may feel alone, as if no one else struggles in the same way. But it may actually be a rather common problem.

So, what would God have us do? Continuing to worry and attempting to fix what cannot be fixed just leaves us tired, sad, and drained. We have little energy for other pursuits that might give us joy. Surely that isn't God's plan for us.

We can pray for what we think will solve the problem, but God may not choose to grant that request. There could be countless reasons why. Perhaps a quick resolution would actually cause additional damage to us. Or maybe he wants us to start down a different path. All we know is that we're still hurting.

Perhaps our best choice is to accept reality. When circumstances are outside our control, it may be a relief to make peace with "what is." We can finally stop fretting and pursue a fresh perspective.

In the midst of every trial, there are still flowers, songs, and poems waiting to be enjoyed. The smile of a loved one continues to delight. As we set aside our frustration with the unsolvable, we're free to find joy in the special things God has for us.

You have allowed me to suffer much hardship,
but you will restore me to life again
and lift me up from the depths of the earth.
Psalm 71:20 (NLT)

Be Still
for a
Silent Moment with God

Digging Deeper

Do you have a seemingly unsolvable problem? What is it?

How might your solution and God's way differ?

How can you make peace with reality?

Prayer for Today

Sometimes I'm so frustrated. No matter what I do, I'm stuck in situations that I can't seem to change. If you don't choose to transform my circumstances, God, there's no way I can either. Help me accept reality. Wrap your arms around me and give me peace. Amen.

Your Thoughts

୬

When we bravely share our stories
to help another heal, we reflect Christ.

Living the Wounds

Heal me, LORD, and I will be healed;
save me and I will be saved,
for you are the one I praise.
Jeremiah 17:14 (NIV)

Henri Nouwen has been hailed as a "wounded healer." He even wrote a book by that name. But he's not the only one. Many of us also bear that title.

What is a wounded healer? It's a person who has felt and worked through much pain. Looking honestly at the sorrows and difficulties of life is never easy. Mending a soul can be an agonizing journey. But such a person is then able to transcend personal adversities and share in the healing process of others.

Wounded healers bring wholeness by sharing in the personal journey of those who are struggling. Often a common experience, combined with a caring and empathetic manner, can give new hope to people navigating their own challenges.

This takes much courage. Sometimes we'd rather run from our wounds than truthfully face our struggles. We shove them out of sight as far as possible, presenting a happy face to the world. We lock our painful and fractured history into a small, dingy room, never to be opened to the light. But doing so won't help us or anyone else.

When we honestly speak with trusted friends about the pain in our lives, we open doors for God's grace. When we live in the context of our wounds, we open our souls to God's love. When we step out and bravely share our stories to help heal someone else, we reflect Christ.

He heals the brokenhearted
And bandages their wounds.
Psalm 147:3 (NLT)

Be Still
for a
Silent Moment with God

Digging Deeper

In what ways could your struggles be helpful to someone else?

How can you start the journey toward being a wounded healer?

Where do you see God in this vocation?

Prayer for Today

I have struggled and overcome much. Through it all, God, you've never left my side; your compassionate presence sustained me. I'm excited and energized at the thought of becoming a wounded healer. Help me walk alongside another soul in need. Show me how to become a beacon of your presence to others. Amen.

Your Thoughts

❧

The difficult path often
brings us closest to God.

Worth the Struggle

Consider it pure joy, my brothers and sisters,
whenever you face trials of many kinds,
because you know that the
testing of your faith produces perseverance.
James 1:2–3 (NIV)

The process of healing can be dreary and difficult. In the midst of your struggle have you ever said, "Gee, why is this so hard? This takes way too long and causes huge brain damage. Healing ought to be easier!"

You're not alone. But what are the alternatives? Some try to take short-cuts. Others stop midway and give up. This is common when we're eager to finish up and move on. We're busy people, the clock is ticking, and the world rewards those who run the fastest.

But is a short-cut a good strategy? Will it actually restore your life? Probably not. The spiritual life is one area where the harder the struggle, the more likely we are to appreciate the result.

Consider the example of the early church. Because Christianity was illegal, religious ceremonies were held in strict secrecy. It was hard to find any gathering of believers. New converts had to complete a three-year process before receiving communion. During that time, they weren't even allowed to stay for the whole service, and yet they weren't deterred. Their commitment was strong enough to endure even martyrdom.

The healing of our lives and the deepening of our faith often happen under adverse circumstances. What we gain is precious—a restored body, renewed mind, and stronger belief. Often what brings us closest to God is not the easy path, but the difficult one. He's worth it!

Cast your cares on the LORD
and he will sustain you;
he will never let the righteous be shaken.
Psalm 55:22 (NIV)

Be Still
for a
Silent Moment with God

Digging Deeper

What is your most difficult struggle?

Have you tried to shorten it or make it easier? How?

In what ways has greater healing come through adversity?

Prayer for Today

Sometimes I feel so weighed down by all the difficulties on my path. I wish healing could be easier—or at least faster. But I know my struggles, however long, will yield a sweet fruit of wellness and joy in your presence, God. Help me stay on the road to wholeness and health. Amen.

Your Thoughts

❧

Even in the midst of injustice,
we can still fulfill our calling.

Stay the Course

Trust in the LORD with all your heart;
do not depend on your own understanding.
Seek his will in all you do,
and he will show you which path to take.
Proverbs 3:5–6 (NLT)

Do you ever wonder if your life makes any difference? Do you sense one roadblock after another hindering your progress? Or maybe you just feel down and discouraged. The world often appears inhospitable and isolating.

But you're not alone! History overflows with discouraged people and the challenges they faced. In the medieval church, women were marginalized and generally excluded from any meaningful participation. Some even said that since Adam's rib was curved, Eve and all women were bent on evil. That's not exactly a recipe for a free and fulfilling spiritual life!

Similarly, Desmond Tutu of South Africa, at the time he was consecrated as a bishop, could not vote in his country because of his race. Any white 18-year-old could vote, but Tutu, a black Nobel Laureate, could not. So how did he respond? He simply concentrated on the work God had given him.

Perhaps that's the real answer to the challenges and inequities of life. There are some things we can't personally change. Attitudes of prejudice and animosity are all too common in our world. But even when injustice affects us, we can still fulfill our calling.

We may face circumstances that hinder our efforts to follow God's plans for us. But let's keep walking. Throughout history, that's what true giants of the faith always did. They stayed the course.

Why am I discouraged? Why is my heart so sad?
I will put my hope in God!
I will praise him again—
my Savior and my God!
Psalm 42:11 (NLT)

Be Still

for a

Silent Moment with God

Digging Deeper

Describe an obstacle you face that seems insurmountable.

What does this barrier prevent you from doing?

How can you continue on your path, hand in hand with God?

Prayer for Today

Sometimes I feel crushed by worries and struggles I didn't cause. But over the centuries, your followers have often faced difficulties not of their making. Somehow, they were able to persevere. God, help me follow their example as I walk along the road you have chosen. Be with me always. Amen.

Your Thoughts

⍦

Who you were at the beginning
is not who you will be at the end.

Now Departing at Gate One

And my God will meet all your needs
according to the riches of his glory in Christ Jesus.
Philippians 4:19 (NIV)

Do you long for an exciting new job, but worry that you aren't up to the challenge? Or maybe you have a yearning to do something great or deepen your spiritual life, but you don't think you're that kind of person?

Suppose you went on a long journey, perhaps for several years. When you got back home, would you still be the same person you were when you left? Probably not. You would return brimming with energizing experiences and new maturity. Who you were at the beginning is not who you will be at the end.

Some aspects of your life today probably seemed impossible just a few years ago. Back then, your outlook was governed by what you felt able to do. But as you've grown and accepted new challenges, your world is now expanded.

It's a mistake to think we can't do something wonderful tomorrow, just because we aren't ready today. It's a common delusion. When we believe it, we deny our potential for growth and God's power.

Perhaps it's time to start that far-reaching project or embark on a life-changing path of healing. Sure, we're not ready today for what's in store tomorrow. But God will make certain we're prepared by the time we arrive. So go ahead and catch the plane of life. What are you waiting for?

Take delight in the LORD
and he will give you your heart's desires.
Commit everything you do to the LORD.
Trust him, and he will help you.
Psalm 37:4–5 (NLT)

Be Still
for a
Silent Moment with God

Digging Deeper

Describe something new you'd like to start doing.

What's keeping you from jumping right in?

How can you trust God to prepare you to finish it?

Prayer for Today

There are times when I have trouble moving ahead. I worry that I'm not healed enough or prepared enough to meet the challenge. But I've forgotten your promises to me, God. I know you will change me as we journey together. When the future arrives, you and I will be ready to meet it. Amen.

Your Thoughts

ॐ

As you open yourself completely to God,
you'll discover who you really are.

A Life of Light

*Do you not know that your bodies
are temples of the Holy Spirit, who is in you,
whom you have received from God?*
1 Corinthians 6:19 (NIV)

Have you ever met someone who glows? Who always seems to have the light at his or her back? There's something unusual about such a person. What is it?

Perhaps the difference is that these folks have come to terms with their life struggles. They accept who they are, where they are, and limitations they can't change. They're able to live in freedom, enthusiasm, and joy. In spite of their problems, they inspire hope in all they meet.

I've also met people who seem to radiate the Holy Spirit. There is something distinctive about their faces, their eyes, their countenance. They look as if God is whispering in their

ears, even as they listen to others. A special grace has gently
caressed their cheeks.

As we meet and overcome significant life challenges,
something inside is changed. Our struggle may require
a super human effort and take a long time—seemingly
forever. But in the end, we are transformed.

As we courageously face our struggles, the Holy Spirit
enters in. Our willingness to invite God into the intensity
of our pain changes us from the inside out. A delicate glow
begins to radiate from the depths of our very souls.

Are you drawn to a life of light? As you open yourself
completely to God, you'll discover your true identity. It's
not an easy task—or a quick one. But definitely worth it.

Send out your light and your truth;
let them guide me.
Let them lead me to your holy mountain,
to the place where you live.
Psalm 43:3 (NLT)

Be Still
for a
Silent Moment with God

Digging Deeper

Who do you know that radiates the light of the Holy Spirit?

What do you know about their personal struggles?

How could you follow their example?

Prayer for Today

I've met people who just seem to glow with your light, God. Their countenance is fresh and radiant. I want what they have. Help me to overcome my challenges that I may begin to reflect the Holy Spirit more and more. Let me be a blessing to all I meet. Amen.

Your Thoughts

The Journey Continues

Healing produces scars. Sometimes they're almost invisible; other times they're rough and jagged. But scars are one way to know we've been restored. Likewise, healing may be painful. Again, this can be a sign that we're making progress. Both become badges of honor along the pathway of our journey.

However much we may wish it, healing doesn't happen in a straight line. For most of us, it looks more like a doodle—continuous loops and circles, some high and round, some devastatingly low and wide. But no matter what our doodles look like, we still advance. Our lives may resemble several tiny steps ahead followed by a giant leap back, yet the arc of our progress tilts ever forward.

You and I have had quite a journey together. These reflections have taken us all the way from a phone call that never came to a life filled with sacred light. Jesus has been by our side all along, cheering us on the way.

For most of us, the healing journey never really ends. Rather, it's an ongoing endeavor. During some seasons, we press ahead with vigor. In others, we stop to rest by a cool brook. Though we don't actually arrive, that's okay. With a gracious and loving travel companion like Jesus, we can be content to continue along the path of healing.

Whatever your future journey, and wherever it may take you, I hope you will remember these words from the prophet Isaiah:

> *But those who hope in the LORD*
> *will renew their strength.*
> *They will soar on wings like eagles;*
> *they will run and not grow weary,*
> *they will walk and not be faint.*
> *Isaiah 40:31 (NIV)*

As you and I conclude our time together, let us join together in a prayer of appreciation and hope for the future.

Thank you for this time together, God. In these reflections we've walked paths of sorrow, roads of insight, and highways of healing. Through it all, you have been our constant companion, someone we always count on for encouragement, guidance, and love. Be with us as we continue to embrace our healing journey in the days and years to come. Amen.

May the peace of the Lord be always with you.

About the Author

Lisa Aré Wulf is an award-winning women's devotional author. Her print, audio, and e-books have been finalists in the USA Best Book Awards, Next Generation Indie Book Awards, and Voice Arts Awards. Publications across the country have featured Lisa's articles on Christian living and spiritual growth. She is a recognized speaker who shares her faith journey with transparency and grace.

A graduate of Fuller Theological Seminary, Lisa also holds two degrees from the University of Colorado. She is an adjunct accounting professor, owned a CPA firm, served in elected public office, and was a professional orchestral musician.

Lisa lives in Colorado with her husband, Calvin, and enjoys the beautiful mountain scenery. They have four children and are happy empty nesters.

For more information about Lisa Aré Wulf, please visit LisaAreWulf.com.

Made in the USA
Monee, IL
21 September 2021